There's a
Little Prince
in Every Frog

There's a Little Prince in Every Frog

SPELLS AND CHARMS FOR
FINDING, BINDING, AND
TRANSFORMING YOUR
TOAD (AND LIVING
HAPPILY EVER AFTER)

MIDIA STAR

First edition for the United States, its territories and
dependencies, and Canada published in 2004 by Barron's
Educational Series, Inc.

First published in Great Britain in 2004 by
Godsfield, a division of Octopus Publishing
Group Ltd 2004

Project Editor: Emily Casey Bailey
Project Designer: Anna Hunter-Downing
Illustrator: Victoria Mitchell
Page Makeup: Ana Bjezancevic

Designed and produced for Octopus Publishing
Group Ltd by The Bridgewater Book Company

All inquiries should be addressed to:
Barron's Educational Series, Inc.
250 Wireless Boulevard
Hauppauge, New York 11788
http://www.barronseduc.com

International Standard Book Number 0-7641-5761-2
Library of Congress Catalog Card Number 2003110640

Printed and bound in China

9 8 7 6 5 4 3 2 1

Dedication

*This book is dedicated to all
the princesses out there looking
for their princes.*

Disclaimer

*This book is intended to give general information only.
The author, publisher, and distributor expressly disclaim
all liability to any person arising directly or indirectly
from the use of, or any errors or omissions in, the
information of this book. The adoption and application
of the information in this book is at the readers'
discretion and is their sole responsibility.*

Contents...

Introduction

Definition of a toad: an amphibious creature of the pond.
Another definition of a toad: a man — when he doesn't call, forgets
your birthday, or chooses to watch the NBA play-offs rather than take
you out to dinner.

IT'S NOT JUST UNDER WET stones that the toad lurks, you know. You may well have one sitting right next to you as we speak. Yes, I'm talking about the man in your life who proclaims his undying love for you one minute and hops off to another pond the next.

Men can baffle us, upset us, and leave us perplexed. But help is quite literally at hand in the form of this book. It is ready to show you how, with a little bit of practical magic, you can train Mr. Toad to be your Mr. Prince Charming and do exactly what you want (including remembering your birthday) without him even knowing about it. And it will tell you how to throw him back into the pond if he turns out to be a toad in disguise!

You do not have to be into magic to use this book, nor is any prior experience with magic needed. In fact, all of us already use the power of magic in our lives, often without even realizing it.

This book will help to guide you into a magical relationship with the man in your life. Whether you are looking for a new partner, wishing you didn't always pick toads, or wanting your present man to treat you more like a princess, *There's a Little Prince in Every Frog* will show you how to proceed.

...every princess deserves a prince...

Some Necessary Magical Information

magic-making moons

...the full moon

Some Necessary Magical Information

AS THIS IS A MAGIC BOOK, I should begin by stating a few house rules applying to the craft of magic – love magic, in particular. By following these simple guidelines you will enhance the power of magic in your spells.

Magic is accessible to anyone and everyone. It's not a talent exclusively for "witches." You do not have to belong to a coven; you don't even have to change your religion. Real magic is not about wearing a pointy hat, a pair of fancy Celtic earrings, and heavy black eyeliner. Everyone has the skills and everyone can do it.

There are three main rules that anyone who practices magic should follow – or ignore at her peril:

1. Do as you wish, so long as it harms no other living creature.
2. Do as you wish, so long as you don't interfere with anyone else's free will, especially when it comes to love spells!
3. Whatever you do in life, be it good or bad, returns to you, so be warned!

In other words, do whatever magic you want but never allow it to interfere with or harm another person. The laws of the Universe are such that if someone has hurt you, be satisfied that

he will be "paid back" in some way, at some point in his life. Don't be tempted to take revenge. Revenge spells, particularly those that deal with relationships, eventually come back to you. It's also worth pointing out right here that you cannot do harm by accident. It is your true intention that counts.

Without going into a big history lesson, it's worth mentioning how the craft of magic came about. Witchcraft has been around for thousands of years and is thought to have pre-Christian, pagan origins. The pagans believed in the power of nature. With the help of herbs, plants, trees, and nature in general, they could cure illnesses, drive off enemies, promote the harvest, and make positive things happen in their daily lives.

At that time, every village had what was known as a "wisewoman." She was the local doctor, midwife, veterinarian, and pharmacist all rolled into one (wouldn't you know that it would be a woman!) and would administer lotions and potions as needed.

With the introduction of the Christian religion in Europe, pagans were soon persecuted for refusing to conform, and their beliefs were portrayed as devil worship — hence the excuse for the burning and torturing of witches.

Thankfully, times have changed and, to a large degree, most people accept others for who they are, regardless of what they believe in.

Tools of the Trade

SOME WITCHCRAFT AND SPELL BOOKS insist that you have all kinds of rules and tools if you are going to perform magic. This is not necessary. The individuals who tell you such things are saying so because they like to think they belong to an elite club.

The truth is, you can do magic whenever and wherever you wish. Most of us – yes, even men – do magic without even realizing we're doing it. However, when we become aware of what we are actually doing, we make the magic we already practice more powerful.

The most important tool you need is one that is already within you – belief. If you don't believe that a spell or charm will work, no amount of herbs, candles, or alien words will make it take effect.

The only "tools" you will find in this book are information about the phases of the moon – it has been proven that the moon's position can have a great positive or negative effect on spells – and ingredients that are particularly favorable in relationship magic and can hasten the effect of a spell. These include herbs that are readily available in supermarkets and simple items such as candles, ribbon, feathers, wood, and a range of natural materials. So forget about setting up a magic shrine, investing in a broomstick, or purchasing a white owl called Hedwig; you don't need them.

herbs...candles...ribbons...

Love Spells

YOU CANNOT DO A SPELL to make the hunk in the accounting department suddenly fall into your arms. Relationship magic does not work like that. You can't force people to love you against their own will, and to try will end only in a disastrous relationship.

You can, however, make magic in your life so you no longer have to tolerate a toad. You can take steps toward bringing a suitable prince, one who truly loves you, into your life.

Magic-Making Moons

THE MOON HAS A GREAT INFLUENCE on our lives generally and has even greater influence when we create magic. Without boring you to death with the reasons why, there are nevertheless a few things to look out for when you decide to cast a little practical magic.

The moon goes through eight phases during its 28-day cycle. These are:

> *The new moon – when the moon is not visible*
>
> *The first waxing crescent – when the moon looks like a slim D shape*
>
> *The first quarter – when the moon looks like a half circle in a D shape*
>
> *The waxing gibbous moon – when the moon looks like a football*
>
> *The full moon – when the moon looks like a basketball*
>
> *The waning gibbous moon – when the moon looks like a football*
>
> *The last quarter – when the moon looks like a half circle in a C shape*
>
> *The waning crescent – when the moon looks like a slim C shape*

Here's an easy way to remember your magic-making moon rules: If you want something positive to happen in your life, you will give it more power by doing your spell on a full moon or a waxing moon. If you want something to disappear from your life, you should do a spell during a new moon or a waning moon. So, if you wanted to attract a loving prince into your life, you would do one of the attraction spells during a full or waxing (D-shaped) moon. If, on the other hand, you wanted to send a slimy toad back where he belongs, you would do a banishing spell during a new moon or a waning (C-shaped) moon.

Candles and Days

IT IS BELIEVED THAT SPECIFIC days and candles of specific colors can enhance a spell – speed it up and make it more powerful. Please note, however, that it is not imperative that you do a certain spell on a certain day, with a candle of a particular color, or even under a certain moon phase. The wonderful thing about magic is that you can do it anytime. So long as you believe in it and respect it, it will work just as well as if you did it on the appropriate day – maybe not as quickly, but it will still work for you.

The best days for practicing relationship magic are:

> TUESDAY – for spells to protect you, for example,
> to safeguard you from a bad toad
> FRIDAY – for spells associated with love,
> for example, attracting a prince
> SATURDAY – for banishing something from your life
> SUNDAY – for confidence and success, for example,
> if you need the confidence to ask a man out

The best candle colors to use in relationship magic are:

Pink   Red   Gold

These colors are associated with love, peace, and tranquillity – all the ingredients you need for a magical relationship. If you do a banishing spell, use a dark blue candle, if possible.

P's and Q's (Please and Thank You!)

WE'VE ALWAYS BEEN TAUGHT TO say "please" and "thank you," and magic is no exception. When you finish performing a spell or a charm, no matter how silly it sounds, always say "please." When your wish comes true, say "thank you." You don't have to shout it out loud; you can whisper it to the Universe if you like. But please do mind your P's and Q's.

I Believe

YOU DO NOT NEED TO BE a devoted witch to make magical things happen in your life, including in your love life. You do not have to change your religious beliefs, nor do you have to take on new beliefs. What is important is that you believe that a spell will work. No amount of wand waving will make a spell work if you don't believe that it will.

You would be amazed at the number of women who practice magic in their everyday lives. They are people you meet every day – lawyers, housewives, dentists, organic vegetable growers. You name it, there is a woman out there somewhere doing it – and at the same time making her life magical, and certainly not putting up with a toad in her life!

The woman you meet at the bus stop or at the supermarket checkout may well be making magic in her free time. We don't all dress in black (unless of course it's in fashion again) or run around in the garden naked and chanting rhymes (unless of course we've had too much to drink!).

Princes and Princesses

THERE REALLY IS A PRINCE FOR every princess, and although you may well meet a few toads on the way, you will eventually discover that there are quite a few princes out there for you (with millions of men in the world, you can have your pick). He doesn't have to be Mr. Right so long as he treats you like a princess. In fact, he could be Mr. Kind-and-Caring-for-the-Time-Being, until Mr. Right does come into your life.

Remember, too, that we all change as we grow older. The teenager with the cute dimple you fell for all those years ago would probably not have been the ideal life partner for you ten years down the line. The man you dream of right now might not turn out to be Mr. Happy-Ever-After in a year's time.

The purpose of this book is not to make you think that the prince of your dreams will be the one you will live with for eternity; it's to enable you to stop attracting toads and begin attracting princes who will treat you with the respect you deserve. Real spell crafting is not about making everything fine and dandy and it is not a quick fix for relationship problems. It's not about waving a magic wand and having everything suddenly handed to you on a silver platter. It is a helping hand to achieving magical relationships. Even if you have never done magic before, you will soon see how your life will change for the better.

Now that you have some basic witchy information, we can get on with the fun stuff and banish those toads to the bottom of the murky pond, where they belong!

Banishing and Confidence Spells

...mend a broken heart...

You Might Have to Kiss a Lot of Frogs ...

WE'VE ALL KISSED A LOT OF FROGS. You know how it is: Mr. Charming-Smarmy-Pants knocks you off your feet. Then, three weeks later, he shows his true colors and turns out to be a slimy toad in disguise – and breaks your heart to boot!

Why do we do it? We put ourselves through heartache time after time, until we're sure we're destined to put up with rotten toads for the rest of our lives or live a secluded life on a lily pad made for one. The explanation is quite simple. It's all about the power of attraction and one's sense of self-worth. If you don't think you deserve better than a toad, then that's what you are going to get, time and time again.

But please don't think it's entirely your fault that you keep hooking up with Mr. Croaker of Slimy Pond Road. It's not. Some toads take great pleasure in breaking our hearts, which knocks our self-esteem and makes us feel worthless. Nevertheless, when we're down on ourselves, we send out the wrong signals – desperate signals – to the toads in the pond, and so attract them to us.

In this chapter, you'll learn some banishing spells to get rid of a toad who is ruining your life and some confidence-boosting spells that will help you do better next time.

Please don't confuse banishing with revenge. I know it's very tempting to put a hex on some toad who's just sent you a text message saying that he never wants to see you again, but you should never, *ever* do a spell for revenge. Doing so will only result in unhappiness for yourself.

Regardless of what religion you believe in, the natural laws of cause and effect, known to some as karma, apply to us all. When you do something good, you will receive good in return. If you do something harmful, you receive accordingly – maybe not tomorrow, but at some point in your life, so don't go making a voodoo doll or pouring sugar into his gas tank. Trust me: he will get his comeuppance.

...maybe this time...

Banish the Bothersome Toad Spell

★ ★ ★ ★ ★ ★ ★ ★ ★

This spell is designed to put a stop to a toad who is bothering you, be he an ex, or just a frog whose attentions on you are unwanted!

You will need

A long blue candle
Something personal from the perpetrator
(such as a sample of handwriting, hair from a hairbrush, a photograph)
A few sprigs of rosemary
A heatproof dish or bowl

Timing: For optimum power, do this spell on a Saturday night during a waning (C-shaped) moon. Try not to let angry thoughts come into your head while you do this spell. Okay, so he might be a pain in the derrière, but he is only a man when all is said and done, and your anger at him will only confuse the spell.

What you do

✡ Light the candle and place it on the windowsill in your bedroom. Next, place the sample of handwriting or other personal item in the heatproof dish, next to the candle. Place the few sprigs of rosemary in the dish too.

✡ Concentrate on the bothersome toad (without getting angry!) and repeat the following three times:

It's time for you to move on now and stay out of my life,
I no longer allow you to cause me strife.
Be gone, be gone, be gone. So mote it be.

✡ If the personal item you managed to obtain is paper, a strand of hair, or some other burnable item, set this and the rosemary alight with the flame of the candle. If it is something that will not burn, simply drop a few drops of candle wax onto it, light the rosemary, and then bury the object in the garden.

Burning the personal object tells the Universe that you will no longer tolerate this bothersome toad in your life. Burning the rosemary shows that you have no ill feelings and demonstrates that your life will be as sweet as the herb's aroma.

✡ Allow the candle to burn down as long as you can. Note: if you are going out of the room or out of the house, blow the candle out and relight it when you return. You will soon notice that the bothersome toad is no longer pestering you.

A Quick Confidence Compact Charm

★ ★ ★ ★ ★ ★ ★ ★ ★

When we've been the victim of a toad, our confidence can fall to the bottom of the charts. It's all very well to want to stay under the down comforter forever, listening to old love songs over and over, but you'll never meet your true Prince Charming if you do. This little charm is sure to boost your confidence and have you throwing out those old love letters for good.

You will need

A small, empty powder compact with a mirror inside
A piece of paper cut in a circle to fit inside the compact
A pen with gold or silver ink

Timing: Do this spell on a Sunday when there is a new moon.

What you do

🐾 First, drag yourself out from under that smelly comforter and get dressed! Grab your makeup box and make yourself gorgeous again. Take time applying your makeup and doing your hair, until you feel happy with the way you look. We all have something that is our best quality, so make the most of yours.

🐾 Sit down and write on your circle of paper, in gold or silver ink, all the positive things you can think of about yourself. If you can't think of any, remember the positive statements other people have made to you about you. What was it that attracted your previous partner to you? How many times have you been told how dazzling your smile is? If you really can't think of anything, phone a friend and ask that friend to tell you five of your positive qualities off the top of his or her head. Write these down.

🐾 Paste the piece of paper inside your compact where the powder used to be.

🐾 Look in the compact's mirror and see how lovely you really are. Say six times:

I am a wonderful and confident person now.

🐾 Every time you need a quick confidence boost, open the compact, read your note to yourself, and smile. You will feel 100 percent better every time.

I Will Survive Spell!
★ ★ ★ ★ ★ ★ ★ ★ ★

It's easy for other people to tell you there are plenty of princes in the pond, but when you've just broken up with someone special, it can feel like the end of the world. At times like this you need to be a little bit selfish and administer some T.L.C. to yourself. This little spell won't mend a broken heart — only time will do that — but it will help you cope with life until your prince comes to the rescue.

You will need

Two drops of lavender oil
Two drops of rose oil
Some bubble bath
A few rose petals
A felt-tip pen with pink ink
A box of your favorite chocolates
A glass of sparkling white wine

Timing: Do this spell on a Friday during a new moon, if you can. Choose a night when you can pamper yourself and won't be disturbed.

What you do

❧ First of all, run a bath and add the drops of lavender and rose oil. Don't add them to hot running water, as this will weaken their aroma. Add lots of bubbles and then the rose petals. Pour yourself a glass of wine (you can have red if you prefer) and place a few of your favorite chocolates on the side of the bathtub.

❧ When you feel ready, step into the bath and let the aroma of the oils warm all your senses.

❧ Take your felt-tip pen and draw as many pink hearts as you like all around the bathtub – don't worry, these will wash off; I've tried it!

❧ When you've finished, admire your handiwork and say three times:

I am now free to welcome new love into my life;
I feel vibrant and alive.
This experience just makes me stronger;
I know I will survive.

❧ Congratulate yourself that you have gotten this far without crying or getting angry. Indulge yourself with your glass of wine (pretend it's champagne) and your chocolates. This is the new you, and that frog was just pretending to be a prince, anyway! You can do this little ritual as many times as you like to make you feel alive again.

Mr. No-Good-Toad Spell

★ ★ ★ ★ ★ ★ ★ ★ ★

You know how it is — you know he's a toad, but you think you can change him. Listen, ladies, a toad never changes his warts, and no amount of nagging will make him transform. Sometimes some people are just not good for us, and deep down we know this. If your man is making you miserable and isn't treating you like a princess, then it's time to move on. You deserve better, and you know it! Try this little spell to put him back in the pond, leaving yourself open for someone better.

You will need

One oak leaf
One free-range egg
Some garden twine
A black marker pen

Timing: Do this spell on a Saturday night during a waning moon for optimum power.

What you do

❀ Carefully write the toad's name on the egg with your marker pen.

❀ Wrap the egg in the oak leaf, and tie the garden twine around it tightly.

❀ Take the small parcel outside and by the light of the moon say:

You are no good for me and don't treat me like a princess;
go and find someone more suitable instead.
I banish you from my heart from now on.
So mote it be.

❀ Throw the parcel either into a flowing body of water, such as a river, or into the trash. The egg and oak leaf will naturally decay. As they do, your toad will skulk back under his rock, leaving you free to let a real prince into your life!

Mend a Broken Heart Spell

★ ★ ★ ★ ★ ★ ★ ★ ★

True love rarely runs smoothly, and when the one you love suddenly decides he doesn't love you anymore, your heart can feel as though it is broken in two. This little spell will help the healing process, and in time you will look back and realize what a complete toad he was in the first place.

You will need

One blue candle

A bowl of soil

One matchstick

Some sticky tape

Timing: Do this spell on a new moon, if possible, and on a Saturday night.

What you do

❧ Light the candle and then break the matchstick into two pieces. The break represents your broken heart. Allow yourself time to think about what has happened. You might feel a wave of emotions – distress, hurt, anger. Allow your emotions to flow freely. You might not have had the chance to really think about it before now.

❧ Next, tape the two pieces of matchstick back together with the sticky tape. This symbolizes your heart being mended again. Light the match with the candle, taking care not to burn your fingers.

❧ Then extinguish the match in the bowl of soil and say:

My broken heart is on the mend;
I will soon be free to love again.
Our love was just not meant to be,
although it hurts I am now free.

❧ Give your bowl of soil back to nature by burying it in the ground. This also represents you burying the past. Your broken heart will soon mend and you will be free to attract someone who really deserves you. See the next chapter in this book!

Attraction Spells

...bring me the prince who will be mine...

Some Day My Prince Will Come ...

SOME DAY YOUR PRINCE WILL COME – HONESTLY. And what's more, he will come to you quicker if you follow the advice in this chapter, which is dedicated to helping you attract a prince into your life instead of a frog.

I must first explain a bit about doing love spells. As I said at the beginning of the book, magic is happening all around us, and it's at our disposal whenever we need it. It is not a quick-fix thing; it takes time and patience. So don't expect to do a spell and see a knight in shining armor riding up the garden path the next minute.

The rules of love spells are very, very important, and refusing to adhere to them will only bring you unhappiness.

First, don't ever try to cast a love spell on a particular person. You may well be wild about Brad Pitt, but it's highly unlikely that he's going to ditch Jennifer and fall in love with you when he is already happily in love. If you cast a love spell for a certain person against his will, the result can only be a disastrous relationship for you. So please don't do it!

Second, when you cast a love spell, think about what qualities your ideal prince would have – not *who* he would be like, because apparent princes can often be frogs in disguise. Think about the traits you would like to see in him – kindness, caring, good looks, willingness to treat you like a princess, love for animals, that kind of thing. It's all very fine to idolize a movie heartthrob, but you have no idea what he is like as a person.

Third, don't hurry love. Make yourself a promise that you will no longer attract toads, that you will pamper yourself and enjoy life until your prince does come along. You may well have to test-drive a few to start with, but I promise, he will come along soon.

Now on to the fun part. The spells in this chapter are great to do on a night when you're home alone — a box of chocolates and a bottle of champagne are optional. Or do them with a few girl friends — again, chocolates and the bubbly stuff are optional, but highly recommended!

...only princes come to me; like a princess I will be...

Attract a Prince and Not a Toad Spell

★ ★ ★ ★ ★ ★ ★ ★ ★ ★

*No one wants to deliberately attract a toad into their lives, but we often find
ourselves doing just that without even thinking about it. This spell is designed
to attract only princes into your life, not toads, frogs, or any other slimy creatures,
for that matter!*

You will need

Two pink candles
Two candle holders
A piece of notebook paper
A pen with pink ink
Two drops of rose oil

Timing: Do this spell on a Friday night and, if possible, during a new or full moon.

What you do

☼ Write your name on one candle and draw a question mark on the other; you can do this with an old ballpoint pen or a pin. Rub the rose oil onto both candles and place them in the two candle holders.

☼ Draw a big heart on the piece of paper in pink ink and add two stick people. In the heart write down all the qualities you want in a man – his age, looks, character, and so on. Make sure you write down everything you would like him to be.

☼ Place the candles on top of the piece of paper and light them.

☼ Now visualize, for as long as you can, your prince entering your life. Say:

Goddess of Venus,
this is my plan.
Goddess of Venus,
send me my perfect man.

☼ Allow the candles to burn down, if it is safe to do so.

Four-Light Love Spell

★ ★ ★ ★ ★ ★ ★ ★ ★

The four elements – air, water, wind, and fire – play an important role in spellcrafting. Fire is associated with passion and love and thus is an ideal element to use in a love spell. This spell will put a stop to your attracting toads into your life and will bring you only princes who treat you like a princess.

You will need

Four tea-light candles
Four rose incense sticks
Four feet of pink ribbon
A heatproof tray

What you do

❧ Begin by concentrating on your future love life and on attracting a prince, not a toad.

❧ Stick one incense stick into each of the four tea-light candles. Inscribe the following words into each candle (one word for each candle):

PRINCE COME TO ME

❧ Place the candles in a circle on the heat-proof tray and arrange the pink ribbon around the candles. Light the candles and visualize your prince coming into your life. Say the following only once:

No more toads shall I attract;
in the pond they will go back
Only princes come to me;
like a princess I will be.
So mote it be.

❧ Allow the candles to burn down, unless you're going out.

Love 2 Surf Spell
★ ★ ★ ★ ★ ★ ★ ★ ★

If you're a bit of a techno witch, the following spell will be right up your alley. This simple spell works on the principle that if you tell the Universe something long enough, you create the power for that something to become reality.

You will need

Your own e-mail address

Timing: Do this spell on a Friday night. It sounds silly, but it really does work.

What you do

♔ Open up your e-mail and write yourself a message. The text should read something like:

Your prince is on his way.

♔ Type the message three times and send the e-mail to yourself.

♔ Don't open the message until the next day. This allows time for it to travel around the Universe and silently inform all the princes out there that you are now available.

♔ Repeat this action for the next three Fridays. Continue to live life as normal, but keep your eyes open! Because your message is reaching the entire Universe, you never know when you might bump into your Prince Charming!

Call Me Spell

★ ★ ★ ★ ★ ★ ★ ★ ★ ★

If you've met someone special and you want him to call you, don't sit by the phone all day. Perform a bit of practical magic instead with this easy-to-do spell!

You will need

A telephone
A small piece of pink paper
A pen with pink ink

What you do

☿ With the pen draw a big heart in the center of the paper.

☿ Within the heart write your prince's name five times and draw a picture of him. It doesn't matter if you're not artistic; a stick figure will do.

☿ Underneath the picture, and still within the heart, write the words "call me."

☿ Place this under your phone. You should hear from him within a week. If you don't, do the spell again.

A Soul Mate Charm
★ ★ ★ ★ ★ ★ ★ ★ ★ ★

There are a lot of princes out there for the taking, but not all will be your perfect partner. After the passion of a new romance dies down, you need something more in common than lust to keep a relationship alive. This spell will help you in your quest for not just a lover but a soul mate.

You will need

Two pink candles ★ One four-foot length of pink ribbon
One four-foot length of white ribbon
One four-foot length of red ribbon ★ A few rose petals
A strand of your hair ★ A white envelope

Timing: Do this spell on a new moon.

What you do

❤ Light the candles. Then tie the three pieces of ribbon together at one end with a knot. The white ribbon represents purity, the pink represents your soul mate, the red represents true love.

❤ Braid the entire length of the ribbons together while chanting the following:

Our hearts and lives entwined together;
the man I meet will be forever.
Him in me and me in him,
now let this spell of love begin.

❤ Tie the two ends of the ribbons together, to create a circle of love. Place the ribbons in the white envelope, along with the rose petals and a strand of your hair.

❤ Sit in a quiet spot where you will not be disturbed and visualize your message traveling out to the Universe.

❤ Seal the envelope with a few drops of candle wax and then allow the candles to burn down fully.

❤ Carry your soul mate charm in your purse until the next new moon, and every night visualize him coming nearer and nearer to you. He's on his way!

I Love Me Spell
★ ★ ★ ★ ★ ★ ★ ★ ★ ★

How can we expect someone else to love us if we don't love ourselves? This is a little confidence-booster spell for those times when we feel unhappy with something about ourselves. If you try this spell and learn to love yourself, you will soon have them knocking at your door asking you out!

You will need
A bunch of brightly colored flowers
Five white tea-light candles
A tall mirror

Timing: This spell is designed to make you love yourself even if you are having a bad hair day. It requires a lot of visualization, so do this spell when you know you won't be disturbed.

What you do

♡ Arrange the flowers in a circle on the floor — big enough for you to sit in. Arrange the tea-light candles in a smaller circle within the flower circle.

♡ Place the mirror outside of the circle in such a way that you can see yourself when you are inside the circle.

♡ Sit cross-legged within the circle and carefully light all five candles.

♡ Look at yourself in the mirror and see how beautiful you really are. Forget about that blemish on your chin or your frizzy hair. See your inner beauty. Repeat the following chant five times:

I am beautiful,
no matter what anyone says.
I am filled with love for myself
in every single way.

♡ Close your eyes and imagine yourself surrounded by a warm orange glow. Allow the warm glow to absorb into your body. Feel how warm and wonderful you now feel inside. This is your inner beauty being restored. Allow yourself to simply be here as long as you like.

Action Figure Spell

★ ★ ★ ★ ★ ★ ★ ★ ★

You may have no problem attracting men into your life, but are they the right men for you? If not, then why not design your own ideal man? On the TV show Sabrina the Teenage Witch *you may have seen Sabrina's aunts creating their ideal man out of dough. Well, this is a similar spell. It has been used successfully by a lot of my girlfriends who were fed up with attracting toads instead of princes.*

You will need

One action figure
One set of action figure clothes ★ One white candle
Three pink feathers ★ A red lipstick

Timing: Do this spell on a Sunday night that has a waxing moon.

You can buy an action figure in most toy stores; failing that, borrow one from your little brother. Choose an outfit that you would like to see your ideal man in. This could be a military uniform, if you like men in uniform. Or you could have great fun designing your own set of clothing if, say, you want a man who dresses casually in jeans and T-shirts.

What you do

❤ Before dressing him up, take your red lipstick and write all the qualities you want in your man all over the figure. Think carefully about what qualities you want.

❤ Dress your action figure in the clothes you've chosen, and place him on the windowsill of your bedroom.

❤ Place your white candle next to him and light it. Arrange the three pink feathers around the candle and the action figure and repeat the following:

Goddess of love, I cast this spell
to bring me this prince who treats me well,
to bring me this man who's good and kind;
bring me the prince who will be mine.
So mote it be.

❤ Give the action figure a kiss. Allow the candle to burn down safely. Soon you should see someone similar to your ideal man come into your life.

Binding Spells

...make our love long and strong...

Forever and Ever More ...

WHEN YOU'VE MET THAT SPECIAL Prince Charming, you'll want to hang onto him. This chapter will show you how to do just that. Remember, you can't force someone to stay with you against his will, no matter how long you've been together. Casting a spell to keep someone with you when you know down deep that things are not going as well as you'd hoped only leads to unhappiness for both of you. So please be careful.

Love Superstitions

There are many superstitions surrounding matters of love.
Here are a few of my favorites:

If a girl meets or kisses her sweetheart under the new moon,
it is considered extremely lucky.
If you are thinking about your lover and you hear a cock crow,
it foretells an early wedding.
If you are in love and you fall up the stairs, you might have a bruise,
but it also means that a wedding is in the future!
When writing a love letter, complete it just before the clock strikes
midnight and mail it at the full moon.
Turquoise is a lucky color for lovers, ensuring
a long and happy marriage.
It's unlucky to mail love letters on Christmas Day or on February 29th,
so mail them the day after.
If you drop your letter to your sweetheart while taking it to the mailbox,
you will quarrel the next time you meet.
It's unlucky to wear your wedding ring before
your wedding ceremony.

Sugar & Spice Makes Everything Nice

★ ★ ★ ★ ★ ★ ★ ★ ★

This sugar and spice spell will help make sure you keep your Prince Charming once you've found him!

You will need

One small red apple

One teaspoon of brown or white sugar

A small piece of paper

A pen

A pinch of cinnamon

A piece of string or garden twine

What you do

❧ Take the red apple and cut it into two halves. One half represents you and the other half represents your prince.

❧ Write on the piece of paper your name, your partner's name, and the word "forevermore."

❧ Now pour the teaspoon of sugar on the inside of both halves of the apple, along with the pinch of cinnamon. Place the piece of paper on top of one half of the apple and then put the other half on top of the paper, so the sugar, spice, and piece of paper are inside the apple.

❧ Tie the apple together with the piece of string so it is secure.

❧ Take the apple outside and say:

Goddess of love, this is my call;
make our love forevermore.

❧ Bury the apple in a sunny spot in your garden, in a windowbox, or in a plant pot. All the ingredients are biodegradable. As they slowly disappear, your love will grow stronger and stronger.

Love of My Life Spell

★ ★ ★ ★ ★ ★ ★ ★ ★

This is a lovely spell to do when you are sure that the prince you have met will continue to be a prince and treat you like a princess.

You will need

Two pink candles

Some glitter

A few rose petals

A tree outside, preferably an old oak tree

What you do

❀ First of all, carve your name in one pink candle and your partner's name in the other one. Place these in separate candle holders.

❀ With the glitter draw a big heart around the two candles – this represents the two of you joined as one. Place the rose petals around the candles and say the following only once:

These candles represent you and me;
happy together we shall be.

❀ Allow the candles to burn down.

❀ The following night, take the melted candle wax and the rose petals outside to the tree. Dig a small hole beside the tree and bury the wax and rose petals there. Make sure you leave the tree as you found it; don't go engraving your names on it, please! You will soon notice how happy you are in your relationship.

Back 4 Good Spell

★ ★ ★ ★ ★ ★ ★ ★ ★

A relationship, like anything else in life, has a life span. Sometimes you just know that one is not going to work any longer and that it's best for everyone to end it for good. Occasionally, however, you can regret having broken up with someone you love and wish that you were back together again. This spell will give you that second chance to make it work.

You will need

A photo of you
A photo of your ex
A length of pink ribbon
Ten tea-light candles

Timing: Do this spell on a Friday night when the moon is new.

What you do

♡ First and foremost, think carefully about the reasons why you broke up in the first place and make sure that getting back together is really what you want. Sometimes it's better for both of you to move on. If you feel in your heart of hearts that your relationship deserves another try, then go for it.

♡ Take the photo of you and pierce a small hole in the top. Do the same with the photo of your ex. Thread the pink ribbon through both holes and tie it in a bow.

♡ Next, inscribe the word "reconciliation" into the tea-light candle and light it.

♡ Place the candle next to the two bound photographs and say:

By the power invested in me,
by the power of the Goddess of love,
reconcile me and (ex-lover's name).
Reunite our love forthwith.
So mote it be.

♡ Repeat this spell for the next nine nights, using a new tea-light candle each night. You should soon hear good news from your ex.

Shake -Up Spell

★ ★ ★ ★ ★ ★ ★ ★ ★

It's easy for the couple to take each other for granted or get bored with the same routines. This spell will revive your passion for each other and make sure your relationship stands the test of time. The apple represents Aphrodite, the Greek goddess of love, so it is an ideal fruit for this spell.

You will need

One red apple ★ One teaspoon of allspice
One empty jelly jar with lid
Some salt water ★ A handful of glitter

Timing: Perform this spell during the new moon.

What you do

♡ Chop the apple into small chunks and place them in the jelly jar. Add the salt water, the allspice, and the glitter. Seal the lid as tightly as you can.

♡ Shake the jar and its contents and say the following:

Aphrodite, Goddess of love,
make our love long and strong.
From this day forth,
we will not get bored.
Make our hearts beat as one.

♡ You should soon see your partner in
a different light.

Sensual Success Spell

★ ★ ★ ★ ★ ★ ★ ★ ★

Magic can't change how another person acts, but it does have the power to suggest.
Irritations like leaving his underwear on the floor, or his desire to pick his nose,
can knock passion right out the window. Try this spell to relight your fire.

You will need

A dozen sprigs of rosemary ★ A dozen red roses
Ten pink candles ★ Lavender oil
A bottle of water with a spray attachment

What you do

♡ Find a time when you can arrange to have a quiet night in together. Arrange
the candles in your bedroom and cover the bed with the rose petals and rosemary.
Mix four drops of lavender oil in the spray bottle's water and spray the mixture
onto your bed.

♡ Run a soothing bath for two and add three drops of lavender oil. Say:

Goddess of love, rekindle our passion.
Goddess of love, soothe away our sorrows.
Goddess of love, make this a fresh start.
Goddess of love, so mote it be.

♡ Ask your partner to join you in a romantic bath,
and afterward move to the bedroom and light the
candles. Allow nature to take its course.

A Prince or a Toad?

★ ★ ★ ★ ★ ★ ★ ★ ★ ★

Amid all the passion of a new romance, it can be hard to know if the love of your life will turn out to be a true prince or an old warty toad. A divining rod can let you know if you are destined to be together forevermore or if he's just a toad passing through. Divining rods have been used for hundreds of years to predict the outcome of any problem or situation and are an accurate way of predicting the future of your love life.

You will need

Your own ring or a pendant
A chain

What you do

❦ Place the ring or pendant on the chain and hold the chain between your index finger and thumb. Rest your elbow on a table and let the pendant dangle freely.

❦ First, you need to distinguish between yes and no answers. To do this, close your eyes and whisper to the pendant a question that calls for a yes answer, such as "Is a ball round?" You may have to whisper the question a few times. Open your eyes and see how the pendant is moving. It may move from side to side, or it may swing in a circle. This is your yes answer. Make a note of it. Stop the pendant from swinging and hold it tightly in your hand for a moment. Now close your eyes again and ask the pendant a question that requires a no answer, such as "Is the sun cold?" Again, watch which way the pendant swings and make a note of it. This is your no answer.

❦ Now you can ask as many questions as you like about your love life and your present partner. Always ask questions that can be answered with a simple yes or no. Each time, first hold the pendant in your hand for a moment and concentrate on the question you have in mind.

❦ To find out if your current man is the best man for you, ask the question, "Is (*name of person*) the right man for me?" Watch which way the pendant swings and check your notes to see if the answer is a yes or a no. You will soon find out who you should and shouldn't be spending your time with.

CHAPTER FIVE

Partnership Spells

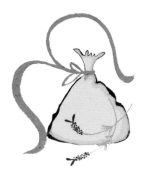

...this magic mix will bring happiness,

laughter, and love forevermore...

First Comes Love, Then ...

THIS CHAPTER IS DEDICATED TO when you finally meet your Prince Charming and decide you would very much like to marry him. Marriage can be quite different from living with your partner – suddenly you're not just an individual but one half of a couple. Married life can also be stressful at times, and silly arguments can erupt over the smallest things. When you have to accommodate your partner on so many issues, it can seem a bit overwhelming. The spells and charms in this chapter will ensure that your marriage starts out the way you want it to and that your married life is happy and harmonious for always.

Who Will You Marry?

Here are some popular superstitions you might like to try before declaring "I do":

☿ Peel an apple carefully so the peel does not break. Throw the peel over your left shoulder with your right hand. The shape of the peel assumes the initial of your future husband's first name.

☿ Take a small piece of wedding cake (not yours) and pass it three times through a wedding ring. Place the cake under your pillow. That night you will dream of your future husband.

☿ Take a photograph of the one you love and hold a ring in front of it on the end of thread. If the ring moves in a circle, you will marry the person in the picture soon. If it moves back and forth, it's unlikely that you will marry him.

☿ Deal a pack of playing cards, one by one and face up, to a circle of your girlfriends. The woman who receives the King of Hearts will be the first to wed.

☿ If you're lucky enough to find a four-leaf clover, place it in your right shoe. The next bachelor you meet will become your husband.

☿ In an otherwise darkened room, place a single lighted candle in front of a mirror. Peer into the glass while you take a bite of apple. It is said that you will see the face of your husband-to-be over your shoulder.

A Happy Lifetime Charm
★ ★ ★ ★ ★ ★ ★ ★ ★

This spell is exclusively for a bride-to-be and should be performed the night before your wedding. Yes, I know you'll be feeling like a bag of nerves, but this spell will bewitch your intended and result in your having truly happy times together.

You will need

A handful of lavender
A handful of mint leaves
A handful of allspice
Two red rose petals
A rectangle of pink fabric
(6 inches x 4 inches [15 cm x 10 cm])
A yard of pink ribbon
Two drops of lavender oil

These ingredients represent all you need for a successful marriage – the lavender represents good health, the mint leaves represent prosperity, the allspice represents a spiced-up love life, and the red rose petals represent the strong love between you and your partner.

What you do

❦ Mix all the ingredients together in a small bowl. As you stir them together say the following:

This magic mix will bring magic to our marriage.
This magic mix will bring happiness, laughter, and love forevermore.

❦ Now with the fabric make a small pouch to hold your magic mix. Fold the material in two to form a 3 inch x 4 inch (7 cm x 10 cm) rectangle, and sew up the open 4 inch side and one 3 inch side to form a pocket. Fill the pocket with your magic mix and tie the top together with the piece of pink ribbon. On the eve of your wedding day, place the pouch under your pillow. The lavender alone will help you to sleep well and absorb any negative thoughts or worries you may have for the following day.

❦ On the morning of your wedding, drop two drops of lavender oil into a basin of warm water and wash your face.

❦ Make sure that when you leave your home for the wedding you take your magic pouch with you. Place it somewhere where only you know it is – in your garter belt, in your flowers, or attached to the inside of your dress. You are guaranteed to have a wonderful wedding and a blissful marriage with your new husband.

Wedding Day Worries Spell

★ ★ ★ ★ ★ ★ ★ ★ ★

It's understandable for you to be anxious about your forthcoming wedding. Will the caterers turn up? Will the cars arrive on time? Will the in-laws behave themselves? Every bride has a mile-long list of worries just before her wedding day. Try not to agonize too much. Do this spell and forget all the worries and just enjoy your day!

You will need

A gold candle
A pink candle
A blue candle

Timing: Do this spell on the Saturday night before your wedding.

The gold candle represents everything running smoothly for your wedding day. The pink candle represents your love and commitment to your partner. The blue candle represents banishing of any anxiety or worries leading up to the big event.

What you do

☿ Find a quiet time where you will not be disturbed and can concentrate quietly for half an hour. Relax in a wonderful, aromatic bubble bath, then wrap yourself in a warm terrycloth robe. Sit for a while and think about your big day ahead and the worries you have been having about things going wrong.

☿ Light the gold candle and say:

This candle will ensure that everything runs smoothly on my wedding day.

☿ Light the pink candle and say:

This candle will seal the love between me and (partner's name).

☿ Light the blue candle and say:

This candle will take away all of my worries.

☿ Watch how, when you say the words, the flame rises higher. Now all you have to do is allow the candles to burn down safely and relax, knowing that your wishes have been carried to the Universe and will be granted.

A Forever Talisman

★ ★ ★ ★ ★ ★ ★ ★ ★

A talisman is a powerful piece of jewelry that attracts positive energy. It takes on properties that work as powerful magnets to attract and hold love. To bewitch your partner so that he will always have eyes for you, make this easy charm.

You will need

A gold locket and a length of gold cord or a gold chain
Three drops of lavender oil
A photo of yourself and your loved one small enough to fit in the locket
A small amount of lavender, basil, and rosemary,
chopped very small or ground up

Timing: Do this on a Friday during a waxing moon.

What you do

☿ Place the three drops of lavender oil on the locket and rub them in. Place the photo inside the locket, along with the chopped or ground herbs.

☿ Hold the locket in your hands and visualize yourself and your partner being happy together forever. Say three times:

Our love is forever sealed within this talisman.
May a lifetime of happiness begin.

☿ Wear the talisman around your neck.

Relight My Fire Spell

★ ★ ★ ★ ★ ★ ★ ★ ★

Juggling children's needs and one's own work can take up most of our time — when we go to bed the only thing we want to do is sleep! This spell will relight your fire.

You will need

One acorn ★ Three pink candles
Five drops of lavender oil ★ Five drops of rose oil
A bottle with a spray attachment (an old perfume bottle will do)
One-half cup (8 ounces [225 g]) of natural spring water

Timing: Give yourself the afternoon off and use this time to tidy up your bedroom, take a warm bath, and perform your spell.

What you do

❧ Fill the bottle with spring water. Add the five drops of each oil and shake.

❧ Place the candles around your bedroom and spray each one with the mixture. Also spray the bedsheets and the air of the room.

❧ When your partner arrives, light the candles and say:

Goddess of light,
this is my desire.
Grant me my wish
and relight my fire!

❧ Hold the acorn in your hand for a moment, and then place it under your pillow when you make love.

Maybe Baby Spell

★ ★ ★ ★ ★ ★ ★ ★ ★

It can be upsetting and frustrating when you are trying to conceive a longed-for baby. And the more you think about it, the more strain it puts on your relationship with your partner. The first and foremost part of this spell is to relax your mind about making a baby. It will happen if it is meant to, so try to be patient and don't devote every hour of the day to thinking about it; studies have found that this doesn't help. For that extra bit of help, do this spell prior to making love with your partner.

You will need

One pink candle
One green candle

What you do

☼ Light the two candles. The pink candle represents the love between you and your partner. The green candle represents fertility.

☼ Say the following twice:

Goddess of the night, grant me my wish,
give me a child this full night.
A strong and healthy child will be granted to me.
So mote it be.

☼ Make love to your partner that night and repeat the spell the following month on the full moon.

Bubbly Love Spell
★ ★ ★ ★ ★ ★ ★ ★ ★

This little spell comes from the Caribbean and is designed to inspire and enhance lovemaking or enchant a lover. Use it if you want to spice up your love life and keep it spiced!

You will need
Three pink candles
A cheap bottle of bubble bath
The following essential oils:
Patchouli ★ Orange ★ Cinnamon ★ Clove ★ Lavender

Timing: Do this spell on a full moon.

What you do

☿ Open the bottle of bubble bath, pour two drops from each of the oils into the bubble bath, and stir with the end of a spoon or a stick.

☿ Mix together a small amount of each oil, rub the three candles with this blend, and allow to dry for a minute or two. Place the candles around your bathroom, light them, and then turn out the electric lights.

☿ Say out loud the name of the person you love a hundred times as you run yourself a bath. Pour two capfuls of your new bubble bath into the warm, running water.

☿ Invite your lover to share your bath. You should see passion return to your love life very soon.

Keeping Lover Faithful Spell

★ ★ ★ ★ ★ ★ ★ ★ ★

It's a horrible feeling to think that your true love might be unfaithful to you; but temptation is out there, and he's just a man, after all! If you're at all worried that your prince might wander, try this quick spell to keep him faithful to you.

You will need

Seven teaspoons of sugar
One teaspoon of powdered ginger root
One teaspoon of cinnamon
A pink ribbon
An empty glass bottle or jar
One-half cup (8 ounces [225 g]) of rosewater –
available in most health stores
One teaspoon of red glitter

What you do

❀ Fill the jar almost to the top with the rosewater. Mix the ginger, cinnamon, sugar, and glitter into the water, and stir as you say the following:

Goddess of love, this is my call:
Keep my lover faithful forevermore;
keep my prince forever true.
This is my wish from me to you.

❀ Place the lid on the bottle or jar. Tie the pink ribbon around the neck of the bottle or jar and store it under your bed. Your lover should have eyes only for you.

Stray Lover Charm

★ ★ ★ ★ ★ ★ ★ ★ ★

Men often find it hard to commit and occasionally wander elsewhere. If you have a Prince Charming who occasionally strays from home, this charm will ensure that he returns. Remember, you can't force someone to love you, and if he continues to roam, then he isn't worthy of your love. This spell will suggest to him that he is with a princess; it won't force him to stay if he doesn't want to.

You will need

Five red candles
A photograph of your loved one
A teaspoon of honey
A teaspoon of cinnamon powder
A red cloth

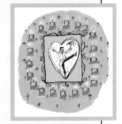

Timing: Do this spell on a Friday night.

What you do

❧ Arrange your candles in a circle and smear them with the honey and cinnamon powder. Place the photograph of your loved one in the circle and light the candles. Say five times:

Lord and lady, may my love be returned to me for good.

❧ When the candles have burned down, place the photo in the red cloth along with the cold wax from the candles. Place the bundle under your bed. Your prince should return home soon.

Champagne Love Spell

★ ★ ★ ★ ★ ★ ★ ★ ★

This little spell is designed to make your relationship sparkle forever!

You will need

The petals of three red roses
Three oak leaves
A bottle of champagne or sparkling wine

What you do

✿ Open the champagne and place the rose petals inside the bottle. Leave in the refrigerator for at least three hours.

✿ Run yourself a warm bath and add the oak leaves to it. Strain the champagne and toss the rose petals into the bath.

✿ Pour yourself and your partner a glass of champagne or wine, add some of it to the bath, and sip the remainder while bathing. It might take a bit of convincing to get your prince to jump into a bath of oak leaves, rose petals, and champagne, but assure him that he will have a night to remember!

✿ Oak leaves act as a natural soap, so you can wash yourselves as nature intended and have a bit of fun at the same time.

Burn, Baby, Burn Spell

★ ★ ★ ★ ★ ★ ★ ★ ★

This nine-day spell will make him burn with desire for you!

You will need

One long pink candle
Lavender oil
Nine sewing pins

Timing: Do this spell on a Saturday night.

What you do

❧ Take one pin and engrave eight equally spaced lines down the length of the candle. This will give you nine sections. Place a pin in the center of each section – one in the first section at the top, and so on right down to the bottom.

❧ As you push each pin into the candle, say your partner's name. Set the candle upright in a holder, light it, and say:

Burn, baby, burn.
Our love will turn into passion
and burn, baby, burn.

❧ Allow the candle to burn down to
the first line and then blow it out. Repeat
for the next eight nights. After the ninth
night you should notice a difference in
your partner's passion for you.

Transforming and Removing Spells

...Goddess within, Goddess without,

make a circle all about...

Is He a Toad in Disguise?

IT WOULD BE A WHOLE LOT easier if men walked around with a label that said either "Prince" or "Toad" around their necks. Unfortunately they don't, and it's only by experience that we eventually figure out who the real princes are and who are just toads in disguise.

When you discover you've actually got a toad disguised as a prince, it can be more than upsetting. And if you've been duped for a long time, it can be quite traumatic and affect everything else in your life.

If this has happened to you, refrain from becoming a man hater – they're not all toads out there! – and try not to take revenge. As I mentioned earlier, revenge will come back to you at some point in your life, and in all honesty, is he really worth all the energy it would take to get back at him?

The spells in this chapter are designed for those times when your Prince Charming turns out to be less than charming. The aim of this chapter is to help you to get over the hurt, anger, pain, and distress and get on with living *your* life to the fullest.

...act like a prince or go back to the pond...

Back to the Pond You Go Spell

★ ★ ★ ★ ★ ★ ★ ★ ★

Whether you discover he's been playing away from his castle or he is just plain horrible to you, this spell will send him back where he came from and he won't bother you again.

You will need

One tall dark blue candle
A strand of the toad's hair (obtain this from a hairbrush)
A photograph of the toad
A black permanent marker pen

Timing: Do this spell on a waning moon at midnight on a Saturday.

What you do

☼ Take the photograph and, with the pen, draw all over the toad's face – you can have great fun giving him Mickey Mouse ears, a mustache, and a face like a pizza.

☼ Place the hair across the photograph and light the candle. Say three times:

You are no longer wanted in my life.
I no longer tolerate your behavior.
This spell will banish you from me.
Get out and do us both a favor.

☼ Allow the candle to burn down safely. The following morning take the photograph and the hair and throw it into a trash can that is due to be emptied. This should ensure that the toad will be in your life no more.

Remember I'm Special Spell

★ ★ ★ ★ ★ ★ ★ ★ ★

You're a princess, right? And a princess should expect her man to act like a prince, right? If he always forgets your birthday and anniversary, or if he hasn't taken you out for quite some time, this spell will help to jog his little memory!

You will need

A calendar
A pad of Post-It notes
A red marker pen
A gold candle

What you do

🐾 With the pen mark on the calendar all the dates that are important to you, such as your birthday, the first time you met, your anniversary, and so on.

🐾 When you've gone through all the months on the calendar, write each important date on a separate Post-It note and stick them up where he will see them.

🐾 Light the gold candle and say once:

You will remember what is important to me
from this day forward and forevermore.
So mote it be.

🐾 The message you send out to the Universe will ensure that he never forgets those special dates. The visual reminders will help him to know what is important to you.

When He Belongs to Someone Else Spell

★ ★ ★ ★ ★ ★ ★ ★ ★

*There's no excuse for a married man to
dupe you, claiming that he's single and
available. To find out that he has a wife
at home can be devastating. You cannot
force someone to stay with you, and if
he's truly as unhappy with his life at
home as he might claim, wouldn't he
have left already? You deserve better
than to share a man who, when all is said
and done, is no better than a toad. If he
can lie to and cheat so easily on his own
wife, he can do the same to you. This
spell is to banish the married man from
your life until he realizes that he can't
have his cake and eat it at the same time.*

You will need

A red balloon

A permanent marker pen

A piece of paper

Timing: Do this spell on a Saturday, preferably on a windy day.

What you do

- Take the piece of paper and draw a picture of the toad who has been deceiving you. Then draw a big cross through the picture to represent that you are not prepared to be a mistress to him anymore.

- Roll up the paper and push it into the balloon. Blow up the balloon so it's full of air. The rolled-up paper will rattle around inside.

- Take the balloon outside. As you release it say these words:

I will not be party to this game of yours.
Go back to where you belong and sort your own life out
before you enter my life again.
So mote it be.

- Make sure you inform your married man that you will no longer tolerate sharing him. He will either come back to you as a free man or remain where he is.

A Happy Parting Spell

★ ★ ★ ★ ★ ★ ★ ★ ★

Sometimes things don't go according to plan in our love lives, and it's often better to cut our losses and start again than to make everyone, yourself included, miserable forevermore. First and foremost, don't blame yourself if your marriage hasn't worked out as you had once hoped. People grow away from each other, and things change. If you're really unhappy, get out and find happiness with someone else. This spell will ensure that if you are separating or going through a divorce, it will be a happy parting.

You will need

A photocopy of your marriage certificate

A black candle

Two small pebbles

A bowl of water

One-half cup (8 ounces [225 g]) of natural spring water

Timing: Do this spell on a waning moon or a new moon. Try not to feel negative when doing this spell. Do it when you have the time to relax. Forget about the arguments and anger that have built up over time and focus on the fact that this is a new start for you.

What you do

☿ If you are right-handed, light the candle with your left hand; if you are left-handed, light it with your right hand. Then fill the bowl with the spring water and place the photocopy of your marriage certificate in the bowl.

☿ Pick up one pebble in your right hand – this represents you – and the other pebble in your left hand – this represents your partner. Concentrate on the two pebbles for a moment. They should begin to feel warm in your palms. When you feel the heat radiating in your hands, say the following:

Like these pebbles we go our own ways.
We will remain friends forevermore,
and we will each find happiness elsewhere.
So mote it be.

☿ Drop the pebbles into the bowl. Place the bowl on the windowsill overnight and leave the candle to burn down.

☿ The following day, retrieve the two pebbles and take them outside. Find a natural area, such as a field or woods, and throw one pebble in one direction and the other in the opposite direction. Throw the photocopied certificate in the trash, and pour the water onto a favorite plant in your house or garden. The spell is now complete and you should have a happy and amicable parting.

Wart Remover Spell

★ ★ ★ ★ ★ ★ ★ ★ ★

No one is perfect, but when his annoying habits begin to affect how you feel about him, then it's time to apply a little practical magic. This spell banishes all those bad habits — yes, even his desire to play air guitar to his favorite heavy metal band!

You will need

One teaspoon of black pepper ★ One teaspoon of cinnamon
One teaspoon of sugar ★ One teaspoon of mixed herbs
A dish to hold the above ingredients ★ Three pink feathers

Timing: Do this spell on a waning moon. This spell requires a windy day.

What you do

☿ Add the ingredients to the dish one at a time. As you mix the ingredients, say:

Bad habit, banish.

☿ Stir the mixture with one of the pink feathers and visualize your prince's bad habits being mixed in as well. Place the feathers in the dish and take it outside.

☿ Find which way the wind is blowing. Throw the entire contents into the wind and say:

Elements of the Wind, carry these bad habits far away so that they may never find their way home again.

☿ Turn around clockwise three times and leave it to the Universe to sort out the problem.

Mend Your Ways Spell
★ ★ ★ ★ ★ ★ ★ ★ ★

All relationships have their ups and downs, and after being together for a while we can often feel taken for granted by our partners. This spell will help to ensure that he turns back into the prince you used to know and treats you like a princess again.

You will need

One teaspoon of honey ★ One teaspoon of sugar
One teaspoon of ground ginger
One teaspoon of allspice ★ One oak leaf

What you do

❦ Mix the sugar, allspice, and ginger together in a bowl, and pour in the honey. When the mixture becomes a thick paste, smear onto the leaf. The sugar and honey will add sweetness to your life, the ginger and allspice will spice up your love life, and the oak leaf will carry your desire across the Universe.

❦ Take your oak leaf to a river or stream. Stand on the bank, or on a bridge over the water, and say the following:

Body of water, take my wish to the Universe.
Grant me that (partner's name) *will mend his ways*
and treat me as I deserve to be treated.
So mote it be.

❦ Close your eyes and count backward from 10 to 1, then throw the oak leaf into the water. Leave without looking back.

Protection Spell
★ ★ ★ ★ ★ ★ ★ ★ ★ ★

I wondered whether to put this protection spell in or not, and when I read that domestic violence accounts for nearly 25 percent of all violent crimes, I felt that it should be included. Obviously, not all men are inclined to hurt women, but there are a few despicable toads out there who do so on a daily basis. First and foremost, if you have experienced domestic violence or are going through hell right now, please, please *seek help from the appropriate authorities. This visualization spell is designed to protect you from harm.*

You will need

A quiet place where you can relax undisturbed

Timing: Do this spell whenever you need strength, courage, and protection.

What you do

❧ Sit quietly for a moment and try to block out any outside noises, such as traffic. Imagine yourself in a golden bubble. The bubble is made out of bulletproof glass and is unbreakable except by you. Only you have the power to break it, no one else. Inside the bubble it's serene and you feel safe and protected. This is your protection bubble, and no one can hurt you in here. Use your mind to make yourself feel as powerful and strong as you possibly can. Stretch your arms out and feel the sides of the golden bubble. They're flexible, but no one can break them. Stay within your bubble as long as you are able. Enjoy the calmness of your own personal space and know that you can jump back into your bubble whenever you want to. Say the following:

Goddess within, Goddess without, make a circle all about.
Keep good in and evil out, Goddess within, Goddess without.

❧ This rhyme will ensure that the Goddess will protect you from now on. Whenever you feel vulnerable or find yourself in a difficult situation, whisper the rhyme to yourself. I guarantee it will work. Remember that if you need to escape, you can create your golden bubble again and go inside it.

❧ This spell is not an alternative to seeking help. You should never, *ever* tolerate mental or physical abuse in your life, and you should always seek help immediately if you feel that you are in any danger. A man is not a prince if he treats you abusively.

CONCLUSION

Witchy Wisdom

How Long Does It Take?

MANY BEGINNERS AT SPELL-CRAFT expect a spell to work
immediately. Or they may hurry a spell to make its results come
more quickly. But I'm afraid they will be disappointed. "Patience"
and "practice" are two key words when making spells. It's not
realistic to do an attraction spell for love and expect a Prince
Charming to appear on your doorstep in a puff of smoke. It takes
time for your wish to travel to the Universe and be granted.

The time span from performing a spell to seeing a result
varies according to several factors, including the words you use,
how much mind power you put into the spell, the will of the
Goddess, the ingredients, and most important, your intention.
Most spells will work – or you should at least sense the situation
changing – within one lunar month (28 days). Or it might take a
few months for you to reach your goal. Be patient; the spell will
work eventually. If the Universe thinks you're not ready for a new
relationship immediately, you may find yourself waiting a while
longer for a new love to enter your life. It may be the Universe's
way of telling us that we need to get over the past before we can
truly appreciate the future.

Spells often surprise us by working a totally different way
than we expected, and sometimes it's not until we look back that
we can see that the spell actually did work. For example, you

might do a spell to attract a Prince Charming into your life and spend the next three months moaning because you haven't met anyone new. Yet in that time you might have found yourself spending more time with your best male friend and beginning to think of him as more than just a friend – a potential Prince Charming! So expect the unexpected at all times.

Magic does not make everything you want just appear; it only increases the probability. And it calls for respect, belief, and some work on your part. Magic can, however, empower you to create the life you want, including your love life. What's more, once you begin to use the magic in your life, as nature intended, other people will soon see a different, more confident you.

Magic won't promote our being greedy and having more than we actually need. People new to spell-craft often wonder why practicing witches don't live in huge mansions, win the lottery on a weekly basis, or even have the ideal men in their lives. The simple answer is because we are provided with what we need, not with what we think we must have.

Making Your Own Love Spells

AS YOU BECOME MORE CONFIDENT in your spell work, you will probably want to try making your own spells. Although I have tried to cover every eventuality in this book, when circumstances arise that call for a spell not provided here, you can design your own spells, and easily.

You can make use of the moon phases and the candle colors and herbs listed in this book and then put together your own words to meet your particular situation. Spells don't necessarily have to rhyme, but they are easier to remember if they do. Just make sure you spend some time considering what it is you require from the spell. If you simply ask to be loved, you might end up with a friendly hedgehog on your doorstep! If you design a spell to make your partner more attentive, you might end up with him being possessive or constantly under your feet!

If you don't have a particular ingredient in the house, or the next full moon is too far away, don't worry, you can still do your spell. Ingredients and moon phases simply enhance a spell. The most important factor in a spell is the power you give to it.

Candles are particularly powerful ingredients in spells, as they represent the element of fire. If you want to do a candle spell but don't have the right color, use a white candle.

White represents everything and is suitable for any spell, be it banishing or attracting.

Sometimes, when all is fine and dandy in your own love life, it's tempting to try and sort out your girlfriend's love life. But don't go and do a spell without her knowing. She may have said she hates her toad of a boyfriend, but that could be because they had an argument. They may well have kissed and made up by the time you set a spell in motion, and she won't thank you for it. If a friend is interested in doing her own magic spells, tell her to buy a copy of this book. She can then make her own mind up about her love life, or you can do spells together.

Love Makes the World Go Around

LOVE MAKES THE WORLD GO AROUND — or at least that's what they tell us! That is how it's supposed to be. Love should be a truly happy, tummy-churning experience, not a constant worry on your mind. If you feel deep down that you're with the wrong person, then staying with him will bring you only unhappiness. Be brave and do something about it. Don't feel guilty. Take that first step. Then take the steps to attract real love into your life. You might have to kiss a lot of frogs on the way to finding your prince, but there really is a prince out there for every princess. And by using this book you will find it easier to attract yours to you!

If you find yourself back on the lily pad made for one for a while, don't be too despondent. First, enjoy your freedom. Second, relax, knowing that this isn't the end; it's just the beginning of a new and very exciting time for you.

Index